Summary

Chapter 0: The Fascinating Universe of Orange Wine

Orange wine, also known as "vino arancione" in Italian, is a type of wine that has been gaining popularity in recent years. It is a white wine produced through a vinification process similar to that used for red wines. This process involves a prolonged maceration of the grape skins along with the must, which imparts the wine with its characteristic orange or amber color, as well as influencing its taste and aroma.

Here are some key points about the fascinating universe of orange wine:

Vinification Process: Unlike traditional white wines, where the skins are removed shortly after crushing the grapes, orange wine production involves leaving the skins in contact with the must for a variable period of time, ranging from a few days to several weeks. This allows the grapes to transfer tannins, antioxidants, and other compounds from the skins to the must, giving the wine its distinctive color and a range of more intense aromas and flavors.

Color and Appearance: Orange wine gets its name from its color, which ranges from golden to deep orange and even amber. This spectrum of colors is the result of the extended skin contact during the vinification process.

Aromas and Flavors: Orange wine can exhibit a unique aromatic and flavor profile, often characterized by notes of citrus, flowers, spices, dried fruit, and sometimes even a slightly tannic component. Variation in production techniques and grape varieties used can lead to a wide diversity of aromatic profiles.

Food Pairing: Due to its structure and complexity, orange wine can be an excellent choice for food pairings. It pairs well with flavorful dishes such as grilled meats, aged cheeses, spicy dishes, and ethnic cuisine.

Historical Origins: Although the orange wine production process has been revived in recent decades, its origins date back thousands of years, particularly in regions like

Georgia and Armenia. In these areas, wine was often produced with extended skin maceration periods.

Market and Trends: Orange wine is gaining popularity among wine enthusiasts and industry experts. Many artisanal wineries and innovative producers are experimenting with this technique, contributing to a wide range of wines with unique characteristics.

In summary, the world of orange wine is a captivating oenological universe that combines traditional techniques with a modern approach to winemaking. Its diversity of colors, aromas, and flavors makes it an intriguing option for wine lovers seeking unique sensory experiences and new gastronomic challenges.

Chapter 1: The Ancient Art of Winemaking with Skins

The ancient art of winemaking with skins, also known as extended maceration or amphora winemaking, is a traditional method of wine production that dates back to ancient times. This process involves leaving the grape skins in contact with the must for a longer period compared to conventional winemaking methods. During this time, the skins release compounds such as tannins, polyphenols, aromas, and colorants into the must, contributing to the creation of a wine that is unique in terms of color, aroma, and structure.

Here are some key points about the ancient art of winemaking with skins:

History: Winemaking with skins is a technique that dates back thousands of years. Ancient civilizations such as the Roman, Greek, and Georgian cultures used this method in winemaking. In particular, terracotta amphorae were often used as containers for fermentation and wine storage, as they allowed gentle permeability that influenced the winemaking process.

Maceration: During extended maceration, the skins are kept in contact with the must for a variable period, ranging from days to weeks. This process allows the must to extract a higher concentration of compounds, such as tannins that give the wine structure and astringency, as well as polyphenols that affect color and aroma.

Terracotta Amphorae: In antiquity, terracotta amphorae were frequently used as vessels for fermenting and aging wine. These containers allowed for gentle oxygenation and interaction between the wine and the external environment, contributing to the formation of the wine's profile.

Color, Aroma, and Flavor: Winemaking with skins can impart a range of colors that span from golden to orange and amber, akin to orange wines. The aromas and flavors resulting from this method can include notes of citrus, dried fruit, flowers, and spices, with a more intense structure compared to wines produced using more traditional methods.

Modern Trends: In recent years, winemaking with skins has been revisited by many modern producers. The technique has been embraced by artisanal and innovative wineries seeking to create unique and authentic wines that harken back to traditions of the past.

The ancient art of winemaking with skins represents a connection to the historical roots of winemaking and offers an alternative and exciting way to create wines with distinctive characteristics. The practice continues to inspire producers worldwide to experiment with traditional methods and preserve ancient winemaking techniques for future generations.

Chapter 2: The History of Orange Wines Through the Centuries

The history of orange wines, also known as orange wine or amber wine, dates back thousands of years and has roots in various wine regions around the world. These unique wines have been produced through vinification processes involving extended maceration of white grape skins with the must, giving them their characteristic orange or amber color and distinctive aromatic and flavor profiles. Here's an overview of the history of orange wines through the centuries:

Ancient Times in Georgia and Armenia: The origins of orange wines trace back to ancient Georgia and Armenia, where they were produced using the amphora fermentation method. Terracotta amphorae were used to store grapes along with their skins during the fermentation process. This method contributed to creating wines with intense colors and characteristic aromas.

Ancient Mediterranean Civilizations: In antiquity, wines similar to orange wines were also produced in Mediterranean civilizations such as Greece and Rome. Amphorae and vinification techniques involving skin maceration were common, resulting in wines with shades of orange color and distinct aromatic profiles.

Developments in Eastern Europe: Over the centuries, the practice of skin maceration winemaking was preserved in certain regions of Eastern Europe, such as Slovenia and Croatia. However, this technique gradually gave way to more modern and standardized production methods.

Rediscovery and Modern Renaissance: In recent decades, there has been a resurgence of interest in skin maceration winemaking, thanks to a new generation of producers embracing traditional and artisanal techniques. These producers have experimented with extended maceration and amphorae, contributing to the trend of orange wines in the contemporary wine industry.

Current Popularity: From the 2000s onwards, orange wines have gained international popularity. Innovative producers worldwide have embraced this practice and experimented with various techniques, grape varieties, and styles, creating a wide range of wines with unique characteristics. These wines have become sought after by both wine enthusiasts and industry experts.

The history of orange wines through the centuries represents a connection to ancient winemaking traditions and a rediscovery of practices that have been passed down over time. The modern interest in these wines reflects a growing quest for authenticity and innovation in the wine industry, where producers seek to create unique sensory experiences through the use of traditional techniques.

Chapter 3:
The Maceration Process: From Crushing to Orange

The Maceration Process in the context of orange wines is crucial for achieving the distinctive color, aroma, and taste of these unique wines. This process involves the extraction of compounds from the skins of white grapes, imparting the wine with its characteristic orange or amber color and distinctive aromatic and flavor complexity. Here's how the maceration process unfolds from crushing to obtaining orange wine:

Grape Selection: To produce orange wines, it's important to select high-quality white grapes. Often, grapes from indigenous grape varieties are preferred as they can offer unique aromatic profiles and characteristics.

Crushing: After harvesting, the grapes are crushed to obtain the must. Unlike the traditional winemaking of white wines, where the skins are removed immediately, in the maceration process, the decision is made to keep them in contact with the must for a longer period.

Maceration: The skins are left in contact with the must for a variable period, ranging from days to weeks. During this time, the skins release compounds such as tannins, polyphenols, and colorants into the must. This contributes to creating the distinctive orange or amber color and imparts the wine with a robust and complex structure.

Fermentation: Fermentation occurs with the skins still present in the must. During this process, naturally occurring or added yeasts convert sugars into alcohol, and in this context, extraction of compounds from the skins also occurs.

Maturation and Aging: After fermentation, the wine may undergo maturation and aging, often in terracotta containers or amphorae, similar to those used in antiquity. These containers allow for slight oxygen permeability and encourage the wine's evolution.

Bottling: Once the wine has achieved the desired profile, it is bottled. Depending on the producer, the wine may be bottled without filtration to preserve its naturalness and complexity.

The final result of this process is an orange or amber wine with unique characteristics. The color can range from light shades to deeper oranges or even amber hues, while the aromas and flavors can span from citrus and floral notes to spices, dried fruit, and minerality.

It's important to note that there can be variations in the maceration process depending on producers and regional traditions.

The production of orange wines is a form of artistic expression for producers aiming to capture the authenticity of the grapes and the terroir through traditional and innovative winemaking methods.

Chapter 4: Traditional Tools: Amphorae and Other Containers

Traditional tools used in the production of orange wines, such as amphorae and other containers, play a fundamental role in influencing the winemaking process and the profiles of the wines themselves. These tools allow for a more intense interaction between the wine and the surrounding environment, contributing to the creation of unique and distinctive wines. Here are some of the traditional tools used:

Terracotta Amphorae: Terracotta amphorae are widely used traditional containers for the production, fermentation, and aging of wine in antiquity. These vessels have porous walls that allow for gentle oxygenation and gradual interaction with the wine. This permeability can influence the wine's maturation and evolution over time, contributing to its unique taste and aroma profile.

Amphorae Qvevri: Qvevris are traditionally buried terracotta amphorae used in Georgia for winemaking. These large buried containers can hold significant amounts of must and grape skins during the fermentation process. Qvevris have thick walls and are buried in the ground, contributing to stable temperatures and influencing the fermentation process.

Wooden Containers: In some regions, such as Slovenia, Italy, and France, wooden containers like barrels and casks can also be used for producing orange wines. Wood can also provide a slight oxygenation and contribute to the wine's aroma and flavor.

Ceramic and Glass Containers: Besides terracotta amphorae, ceramic and glass containers can also be used for the vinification of orange wines. These materials can have different impacts on the winemaking process compared to amphorae, influencing maturation and interaction with the wine.

Mystical and Traditional Use: Amphorae and similar containers can also have cultural and symbolic meanings in certain winemaking traditions. For example, Georgian qvevris are considered part of cultural heritage and symbolize the unity between humans and nature.

The use of these traditional tools reflects the producers' desire to connect with ancient winemaking techniques and create wines that reflect authenticity and terroir. However, it's important to note that the use of such tools requires careful attention to cleanliness, hygiene, and environmental variables management in order to achieve consistent and high-quality results.

Chapter 5: Celebrated Wine Regions for Orange Wines

In recent years, the production of orange wine has gained popularity in various wine regions around the world. These regions have become known for their ability to produce high-quality and distinctive orange wines. Here are some of the celebrated wine regions for orange wine production:

Georgia: Considered the birthplace of orange wines, Georgia has a long tradition of producing wines in amphorae, locally known as "qvevri wines." These wines are made through fermentation and aging in large buried clay vessels, creating wines with unique aromatic and flavor profiles.

Slovenia: The region of Venezia Giulia in Slovenia is famous for the production of orange wines, often referred to as "macerated wines." Here, producers experiment with a variety of grape varieties and techniques, resulting in wines with a range of distinctive aromas and colors.

Italy: In addition to Slovenia, other parts of Italy, such as the Friuli-Venezia Giulia region and Sicily, have also developed a tradition of orange wine production. These wines reflect the diversity of Italian grape varieties and terroirs.

France: Even in France, some regions have begun producing orange wines, often using natural and traditional winemaking methods. Some wineries in the Jura and Alsace regions have embraced orange wine production.

United States: In the United States, some artisanal wineries, especially in California and Oregon, are experimenting with orange wine production. These producers often draw inspiration from traditional techniques, combining them with innovative American approaches.

Elsewhere in the World: In addition to the regions mentioned above, there are orange wine producers in many other countries, including Australia, New Zealand, Greece, Croatia, and other parts of Eastern Europe.

Celebrated wine regions for orange wines are becoming more widespread as producers around the world experiment with this fascinating winemaking technique, contributing to a wide variety of orange wines with unique profiles.

Chapter 6: The Influence of Terroir on Color and Flavor

Terroir, representing the collection of geographical, climatic, and geological characteristics of a specific wine region, plays a significant role in influencing the color, aroma, and taste of wines, including orange wines. The unique attributes of a terroir can contribute significantly to the personality and complexity of these wines. Here's how terroir can impact the color and flavor of orange wines:

Climate: The climate of a wine region can determine grape ripening, influencing the concentration of sugars, acids, and phenolic compounds in the skins. In cooler climates, grapes might be harvested with higher acids and less sugars, whereas in warmer climates, grapes could reach high sugar ripeness. This variation can impact the color and flavor characteristics of orange wines.

Soil and Geology: The soil where vines grow has a substantial impact on grapes and, consequently, wines. Different soil types and geological properties can influence the chemical composition of grapes, including minerals and nutrients absorbed by the roots. These elements can contribute to the complexity and flavor expression of orange wines.

Altitude: Altitude can influence temperature and sunlight available to vines. In higher elevation areas, daily temperature variations can impact grape ripening, contributing to fresher and livelier taste and aroma profiles.

Sun Exposure: Sun exposure of vines can affect grape ripening and the formation of phenolic compounds. Sun-exposed grapes might have thicker skins and more intense colors, which in turn influence the color and structure of orange wines.

Grape Variety: The grape varieties grown in a specific wine region significantly contribute to the taste and aroma profile of orange wines. Each variety has unique characteristics that respond to the specific terroir conditions.

Cultivation and Winemaking Practices: Vine cultivation practices and winemaking methods chosen by producers can amplify terroir characteristics in wines. The use of amphorae, wooden containers, or other traditional methods can contribute to the authentic expression of grapes and terroir.

In conclusion, terroir plays a crucial role in crafting distinctive orange wines. The combination of climate, soil, altitude, sun exposure, and grape variety contributes to the creation of a unique profile of color, aroma, and taste in orange wines. This is part of the fascinating connection between the wine and the territory in which it is produced.

Chapter 7: The Sensory Experience of Orange Wines

The sensory experience of orange wines is a captivating journey through unique colors, aromas, flavors, and sensations. These wines stand out for their distinctive orange or amber hue, which is just the beginning of an experience that engages all the senses. Here's what to expect from the sensory experience of orange wines:

Color: Orange wines are characterized by a wide range of color tones, ranging from golden to deep orange and amber. This color comes from the prolonged maceration of grape skins with the must. Observing the wine in the glass is the first step into the sensory experience.

Aroma: Orange wines can offer a variety of intriguing aromas. Notes of citrus, flowers, spices, herbs, and dried fruits are often present. The aroma can be complex and multidimensional, encouraging further exploration of the glass to capture the different nuances.

Taste: The taste of orange wines is equally unique. The skin maceration imparts a more intense structure compared to traditional white wines. Tannins from the compounds extracted from the skins can contribute to a light level of astringency and a lingering finish. Fruity, citrusy, spicy notes, and occasionally earthy character can be detected.

Structure: The complex structure of orange wines makes them well-suited for gastronomic pairings. The presence of tannins and aromatic complexity can interact with foods in interesting ways, creating unique tasting experiences.

Palate and Finish: The entry on the palate can be initially surprising due to the diversity of flavor profiles. The tannic structure might be evident but also balanced by pleasant acidity. The finish can offer persistence of fruit, spice, and citrus notes.

Evolution in the Glass: Orange wines can evolve in the glass as they slightly oxidize and warm up. This allows discovering new aromatic and taste facets as you drink.

Tactile Sensations: Due to the presence of tannins and a more robust structure, orange wines can provide tactile sensations in the mouth. These sensations can vary from light to moderately astringent.

In summary, the sensory experience of orange wines is a captivating adventure that engages all the senses. Exploring the color, aroma, taste, and complexity of these unique wines requires curiosity and attention. Orange wines are ideal for those seeking wine experiences beyond traditional norms and wish to discover a world of new and exciting sensations.

Chapter 8: From Visual to Gustatory, a Journey through Aromas and Flavors

In this section of the work, I've decided to guide you through a full immersion journey from the visual assessment of orange wine to the complete gustatory experience, exploring the distinctive aromas and flavors of these unique wines:

Visual Assessment: Observe the color: Pour the wine into the glass and carefully observe its color. Orange wines can range from light gold to deep orange and amber. Reflections: Look for reflections that suggest specific shades, such as gold-green or orange-red. Transparency: Evaluate whether the wine is transparent or slightly cloudy, which can be a characteristic of naturally produced orange wines.

Exploration of Aromas: Swirl the glass: Before smelling, gently swirl the glass to encourage the evolution of aromas. Primary aromas: Bring the glass to your nose and search for primary aromas like citrus, flowers, dried fruit, spices, and even earthy or woody notes. Depth and complexity: Seek the depth and complexity of the aromas, searching for different layers of scents that develop as the wine oxygenates.

Tasting Flavors: Taste: Take a small sip and let the wine spread in your mouth. Mouthfeel: Note the mouthfeel, including the sensation of tannins and acidity. Orange wines often present a more robust structure compared to traditional white wines. Primary flavors: Look for the primary flavors you detected in the aroma, such as citrus, dried fruit, and spices. Complexity: Seek additional nuances of flavor that might emerge during tasting. Aftertaste: Pay attention to the aftertaste, which is the persistence of flavors after swallowing. Orange wines often have a prolonged aftertaste.

Tactile Sensations and Finish: Mouthfeel: Evaluate the tactile sensation in your mouth, including the possible astringency of tannins. Finish: Consider how the wine leaves your mouth after tasting. The finish can be dry, fresh, or lingering.

Evolution in the Glass: Observe how the wine changes as it oxygenates and warms in the glass. New aromas and nuances can emerge.

This sensory journey through the aromas and flavors of orange wines offers you the opportunity to explore the complexity and authenticity of these unique wines.

Chapter 9: The Passion and Innovation of Orange Wine Producers

Orange wine producers are driven by a deep passion for the art of winemaking and innovation in the wine industry. The production of orange wine represents a return to ancient winemaking traditions combined with an open-mindedness towards new techniques and creative approaches. Here's how passion and innovation are reflected in orange wine producers:

Respect for Traditions: Orange wine producers often seek to honor ancient winemaking traditions. They are fascinated by the history of amphora winemaking and skin maceration, and see orange wine as a way to preserve and rejuvenate these ancient practices.

Experimentation with Grapes: The producers' passion is reflected in the choice of grape varieties used for orange wine production. They often choose indigenous or less common varieties that can best express themselves through extended maceration.

Natural and Artisanal Methods: Many orange wine producers adopt natural and artisanal approaches in production. This can include using native yeasts, minimal filtration, and minimal use of sulfur. These methods reflect a passion for creating authentic and environmentally-friendly wines.

Exploration of Terroir: Passion for terroir drives producers to explore how geographical and climatic characteristics influence the final result. Orange wines can be a particularly expressive form of terroir, reflecting the conditions of the place where the grapes were grown.

Creation of Unique Wines: Orange wine producers are motivated by creating unique wines that stand out from the crowd. The innovation lies in the balance between tradition and new ideas to create surprising taste and aroma profiles.

Collaboration and Knowledge Sharing: The orange wine producers' community is often characterized by strong collaboration and knowledge exchange. These producers share experiences, techniques, and challenges, nurturing a culture of mutual learning.

Response to Changing Tastes: The growing interest in orange wine is partly driven by the producers' passion in responding to increasing consumer demand for authentic and different wines. These producers embrace changing tastes and strive to offer unique wine experiences.

In summary, orange wine producers embody a fusion of passion for winemaking traditions, a love for innovation, and a deep connection to the land and grapes. Their dedication is reflected in the distinctive orange wines they produce, which continue to capture the attention of wine enthusiasts worldwide.

Chapter 10: The Art of Pairing: Foods that Enhance Orange Wines

Orange wines offer a complexity of aromas, flavors, and structure that makes them intriguing for pairing with a variety of culinary dishes. Their tannic structure, presence of acidity, and unique aromatic profiles allow for bold and surprising pairings. Here are some ideas for pairing foods that can enhance orange wines:

Fish and Seafood Dishes: Orange wines can pair well with dishes based on fatty fish or seafood, such as smoked salmon, raw tuna, or oysters. The wine's complexity can balance the intense flavors of seafood dishes.

White Meat and Poultry: Dishes like roasted chicken, turkey, or duck pair well with orange wines. The wine's tannic structure can contrast the tenderness of white meats and create a harmonious flavor balance.

Fermented and Cured Foods: Orange wines complement fermented or cured foods like hard cheeses, prosciutto, pickles, and kimchi. Their acidity can cut through the richness of these foods.

Spicy and Spicy-Sweet Dishes: The complexity of orange wines can handle spicy or spicy-sweet dishes, such as curries, Mexican or Indian foods. The wine's aromatic character can amplify or balance spicy flavors.

Vegetable and Plant-Based Dishes: Orange wines can pair well with dishes based on grilled vegetables, vegetable couscous, vegan dishes, and complex salads. Their structure and aromatic variety suit a wide range of vegetable flavors.

Dishes with Moist and Earthy Notes: Orange wines can enhance dishes with moist and earthy flavors, such as mushrooms, truffles, or root vegetable dishes. The wine's earthy and mineral notes can harmonize with these flavors.

Sweet and Sweet-Sour Notes: Sweet-sour or sweet-savory dishes, like Asian dishes or sweet-sour sauces, can be complemented by orange wines due to their structure and aromatic complexity.

Artisanal Cheeses: Orange wines can be paired with a variety of cheeses, such as pecorino, gorgonzola, or aged cheeses. Their tannic structure can balance the richness of the cheeses.

In conclusion, the art of pairing with orange wines is open to many creative possibilities. Experiment with different combinations of dishes and wines to discover which harmony of flavors, textures, and aromas you prefer. The goal is to create synergies that enhance both the wine and the food, leading to a complete gastronomic experience.

Chapter 11: Tips for Creating Extraordinary Flavor Combinations

Creating extraordinary flavor combinations requires an understanding of the characteristics of both wines and foods, as well as a bit of experimentation. Here are some tips for crafting pairings that delight the palate:

Balance between Wine and Food: Strive for a balance between the intensity of flavors, acidity, sweetness, and structure of both the wine and the food. Neither the food nor the wine should overpower the other.

Complement or Contrast: Decide whether you want a pairing that complements or contrasts flavors. For example, a wine with vibrant acidity can contrast nicely with a rich dish, while a fruity wine can complement a fruit-based sauce.

Harmony of Aromas and Flavors: Aim to match the aromatic profiles and flavors of the wine with those of the food. Look for common elements or nuances that pair well.

Experiment with Different Food Styles: Venture into a variety of foods, from light dishes to more complex ones. Try pairings with fish, meat, vegetables, cheeses, and even desserts to discover what works best.

Consider the Wine's Structure: The wine's structure, including tannins, acidity, and body, can influence the pairing. For instance, tannic wines can balance the richness of dishes, while lighter wines might suit delicate fare.

Take Terroir into Account: When pairing a specific wine with food, also consider the wine's terroir and try to find foods that reflect or connect with the wine's region of origin.

Guided Experimentation: Arrange guided tastings where you explore different food and wine combinations. Invite friends or family to join and share your findings.

Update Your Notes: Keep notes on your flavor pairings. Jot down what works well and what could be improved to guide you in the future.

Explore with Different Wines: Don't limit yourself to just one type of wine. Experiment with white, red, rosé, and even orange wines to discover your preferences.

Be Creative and Open to Surprise: The art of pairing is open to various interpretations. Be open to unconventional combinations and let yourself be surprised by the results.

Remember that taste is subjective, so what you enjoy might not resonate with someone else. The goal is to have fun and uncover new culinary experiences as you delve into the realm of extraordinary flavor pairings.

Chapter 12: Orange wines in modern winemaking.

Orange wines have had a significant impact on modern oenology, introducing new perspectives, challenges, and trends in the wine industry. Here are some of the key trends and challenges related to orange wines in modern winemaking:

Trends: Rediscovery of Winemaking Traditions: Orange wines have brought attention back to traditional winemaking in amphorae and skin maceration, reviving practices that date back centuries. Diversification of Offerings: Orange wines have contributed to diversifying the wine market, offering consumers a wider range of taste and style options. This has attracted the interest of wine drinkers seeking different experiences. Focus on Terroir: The production of orange wines encourages producers to highlight the characteristics of terroir and the place where the grapes are grown. This has led to greater attention to the connection between wine and the land. Experimentation and Innovation: Orange wines have inspired greater experimentation and innovation in the wine industry. Producers are exploring new grape varieties, winemaking techniques, and maceration styles to create increasingly unique wines. Growing Popularity: Orange wines have become a popular trend, with more and more wine enthusiasts looking to explore these wines. This has led to an increase in their production and availability on restaurant menus and in wine shops.

Challenges: Consumer Understanding: Orange wines may be a novelty for many consumers, requiring greater education and understanding of their unique flavor profiles. Consistency of Quality: Due to complex winemaking techniques and environmental influences, the production of orange wines can be subject to variations. Maintaining consistency in quality can be a challenge. Maceration Process Management: Producing orange wines requires careful management of the maceration process, as timing and temperatures can affect the final result. Control over maceration is crucial to achieving desired outcomes. Hygiene and Bacterial Risks: Prolonged macerations can expose the wine to hygiene and bacterial risks. Proper equipment cleaning and hygiene management are essential to avoid unwanted contaminations. Balancing Tradition and Innovation: Striking a balance between ancient winemaking traditions and modern innovation can be a challenge for producers as they aim to create wines that honor the past while adapting to current tastes.

In summary, orange wines have opened up new possibilities in modern oenology, sparking creativity among producers and enthusiasm among consumers. As trends shift and challenges arise, these wines continue to play a significant role in the contemporary wine landscape, contributing to a broader diversity of tasting experiences.

Chapter 13: Key terms to understand the language of Orange Wine

To fully understand the language of orange wine and engage in conversations about the production, tasting, and appreciation of these unique wines, it's helpful to know some key terms. Here's a list of important terms to keep in mind:

Orange Wine: Amber or orange wine obtained through extended maceration of white grape skins with the must during the winemaking process.

Maceration: The process where grape skins are left in contact with the must during winemaking. Maceration gives orange wines their unique color, aroma, and structure.

Amphora: Clay vessel used for winemaking and aging. Orange wines are often produced in amphoras to honor ancient traditions.

Indigenous Yeasts: Yeasts naturally present in the environment and on the surface of grapes. The use of indigenous yeasts can contribute to more authentic and complex flavor profiles.

Sulfur Dioxide (SO2): A preservative used in wine to prevent oxidation and bacterial contamination. In orange wines, the use of sulfur dioxide can vary, with some producers opting for minimal or no added amounts.

Terroir: The combination of geographical, climatic, and geological features of a wine region that influence the grapes and the produced wine. Orange wines often highlight terroir influences.

Tannins: Polyphenolic compounds primarily found in grape skins. Orange wines can have tannins due to extended skin maceration.

Structure: The sensation of body, tannins, and acidity in the wine. Orange wines often have a more robust structure compared to traditional white wines.

Aromatic Complexity: The presence of various aromas that develop in the wine. Orange wines are known for their aromatic complexity, which can change as the wine oxidizes.

Acidity: A key component in wine that contributes to its freshness and liveliness. Orange wines can have good acidity, balancing structure and complexity.

Evolution in the Glass: The change in aromas, flavors, and tactile sensations a wine undergoes as it's exposed to oxygen and warms in the glass.

Natural Winemaking: A minimalist approach to winemaking that avoids the use of chemical additives and invasive interventions. Many orange wine producers follow natural winemaking practices.

Comparative Tasting: The process of tasting different orange wines simultaneously to compare their characteristics and differences.

Astringency: The tactile sensation of dryness or roughness in the mouth caused by tannins. Orange wines can exhibit slight astringency.

Finish: The persistence of flavors and sensations after swallowing the wine. Orange wines can have a prolonged and complex finish.

These key terms can help you better understand the language and conversation surrounding orange wines. They are essential for exploring and fully appreciating these distinctive wine expressions.

Chapter 14: The list of Orange Wines to taste

The evaluation of "best" orange wines can be subjective and depends on personal tastes and individual preferences. However, I can give you an idea of some labels of orange wines produced by renowned producers that are often considered among the best in their category. Keep in mind that the selection may vary depending on regions and vintages. Here are some names of well-known producers and orange wines:

Radikon: A natural wine producer in Friuli-Venezia Giulia, Italy. Their orange wines are highly appreciated for their complexity. "Oslavje" is one of their most famous wines.

Gravner: Another renowned Italian producer from the Friuli-Venezia Giulia region. Josko Gravner is known for reviving the tradition of using amphorae. His "Anfora" is an icon of orange wines.

Movia: This Slovenian producer is famous for its traditional and natural wines. "Veliko Bianco" is a well-known label of orange wine.

Amphorae Wines: This Georgian producer specializes in wines vinified in amphorae following Georgian traditions. Their "Qvevris" is a highly appreciated orange wine.

La Stoppa: An Italian producer from Emilia-Romagna, known for their orange wine "Ageno".

Grain & Grape: This Australian producer is known for their natural wines, and their "Cosmic Adventures in Sound" is a recognized orange wine.

Radford Dale: A South African producer that produces a renowned orange wine called "Thirst".

Cullen Wines: This Australian producer is appreciated for its sustainability, and their "Amber" is a notable example of orange wine.

Sato Wines: A Japanese producer that makes orange wines using local grapes and traditional methods. Their "Abe no Matsusaka" is known in the realm of orange wines.

alvo Foti: A Sicilian producer known for natural wines, including orange wines like "Vigneri" Etna Bianco.

Angiolino Maule: An Italian producer who was a pioneer in natural and orange wine production. His "Sassaia" is highly regarded.

Matassa: This producer from southern France is known for natural wines, and their "Cuvée Marguerite" is an example of orange wine.

Valentin Morel: A producer from Jura, France, known for natural and orange wines like "Enfant Terrible".

Massa Vecchia: An Italian producer in Tuscany making organic wines, and their "La Mora" is an orange wine to try.

Iago's Wine: A Georgian producer specializing in amphora wines, like their "Chardakhi".

Tenuta Grillo: An Italian producer from Sicily, known for their orange wine "Itaca".

Rennersistas: This Austrian producer is known for natural wines, and the label "Waiting for Tom" is an example of orange wine.

Gabrio Bini: An Italian producer from the island of Pantelleria, known for natural wines, and his "Anfosso" is an orange wine icon.

Tenuta di Tavignano: An Italian producer from Marche, producing the orange wine "Misco".

Remember that personal preferences can vary, so I recommend exploring different labels and producers to discover which orange wines suit your taste best. Additionally, consult specialized wine shops, restaurants, and industry magazines to discover new findings and the latest trends in orange wines.

Chapter 15: Fine orange wines for investment and collection

There are orange wines that can be considered for investment, but it's important to note that investments in the wine industry are subject to risks and require a deep understanding of the market and trends. As with any form of investment, it's crucial to conduct your research and consult industry experts before making decisions.

Some factors to consider when evaluating orange wines as potential investments include:

Producer Reputation: Wines produced by renowned and respected producers in the industry are more likely to maintain or increase their value over time.

Limited Release and Availability: Orange wines produced in limited quantities or in particularly good vintages can gain value over time due to their rarity.

Exceptional Vintages: Outstanding vintages can increase the value of a wine over time, as wines from those years are often considered collectible delicacies.

Artisanal and Natural Approach: Wines produced using artisanal and natural methods may be considered more authentic and desirable for collectors.

Expert Ratings: Positive ratings from wine industry critics can influence the value of a wine.

Market Trends: Consumer trends and interests can influence the demand for certain wines.

Wine History and Heritage: The history, region, and tradition associated with a particular wine can influence its value for collectors.

Furthermore, investing in wine requires a certain level of expertise and knowledge to make informed decisions.

Here are some regions and producers known for producing orange wines that could be considered for investment:

Friuli-Venezia Giulia, Italy: This Italian region is considered one of the birthplaces of orange wines. Producers like Radikon, Gravner, and La Stoppa are known for high-quality wines that may have collection potential.

Slovenia: Producers like Movia and Stoka produce high-quality orange wines and are well-regarded in the world of natural wine.

Georgia: Traditional Georgian orange wines, known as "qvevri" wines, are gaining international attention. Producers like Pheasant's Tears and Iago's Wine might have interesting investment options.

Austria: Some Austrian producers like Rennersistas and Gut Oggau are known for their natural wines and might have orange wines worth considering.

Australia: Producers like Lucy Margaux and Domaine Lucci produce orange wines that have garnered attention for their quality and authenticity.

Other Emerging Regions: Due to the growing popularity of orange wines, other regions around the world are starting to produce these labels. It's worth exploring innovative and respected producers in these emerging regions.

Here are some premium orange wine names you might consider:

Radikon "Oslavje": An Italian orange wine icon produced by Radikon in Friuli-Venezia Giulia, known for its complexity and aging potential.

Gravner "Anfora": A legendary wine by Josko Gravner, produced in Friuli-Venezia Giulia. This wine is often considered a benchmark for orange wines.

Movia "Veliko Bianco": Another renowned Slovenian producer, Movia, produces this premium wine with deep complexity.

Pheasant's Tears "Kisi": This Georgian wine produced by Pheasant's Tears is an example of traditional qvevri wine with unique depth of flavor.

Rennersistas "Waiting for Tom": A high-quality Austrian orange wine by Rennersistas, known for its natural expression.

Domaine Lucci "L'Enfant Terrible": Another Australian orange wine to consider, known for its authenticity and character.

Stoka "Rebula Amber": A premium label from Slovenia, with a natural and authentic approach to orange wine production.

Remember, the choice of wines to store in your cellar depends on your personal preferences, the producers you appreciate, and your intention to age the wines. Always consult industry experts, sommeliers, or wine professionals for specific advice on storage and selecting wines for collection.

Made in the USA
Las Vegas, NV
22 December 2023

83440291R00030